The Smug Bridegroom

For
Annie Hamberger
my mother

The Smug Bridegroom

Robert Hamberger

Five Leaves Publications
www.fiveleaves.co.uk

The Smug Bridegroom
by Robert Hamberger

Published in 2002 by Five Leaves Publications,
PO Box 81, Nottingham NG5 4ER
www.fiveleaves.co.uk

Five Leaves acknowledges financial assistance from
East Midlands Arts

east midlands
arts
making creative
opportunities

ISBN: 0 907123 88 0

Design and typesetting by Four Sheets Design & Print Ltd
Printed by Technical Print Services, Nottingham

Contents

Acknowledgments

Acknowledgments are due to the editors of the following publications in which some of these poems (including some earlier versions) first appeared: *Acumen, Agenda, The Frogmore Papers, Honest Ulsterman, Iron, The North, Orbis, Other Poetry, The Rialto, Seam, The Spectator, Staple.*

'Die Bravely' was published as a sequence in *Acumen*. It was shortlisted for the 2000 Forward Prize for Best Individual Poem.

'Sisters' was a prizewinner in the 1998 Peterloo Poets Open Poetry Competition.

'Pink Triangle' was written as part of a commission for the Poets Are Us, Newark and Sherwood Millennium Project, following a visit to Beth Shalom, the Holocaust Centre at Laxton.

'The Rule of Earth' was a prizewinner in The Poetry Business Book & Pamphlet Competition 2000. It was published as a pamphlet by Smith/Doorstop Books in 2001.

The epigraph to 'Sense of Skin' is from 'Black Waterfall' by John Sewell in *Bursting The Clouds* (Jonathan Cape, 1998). Reprinted by permission of The Random House Group Ltd.

The title and epigraph for 'The Rule of Earth' is from 'The Wings' by Mark Doty in *My Alexandria* (Jonathan Cape, 1995). Reprinted by permission of The Random House Group Ltd.

The epigraph to 'Five Years After' is from *Mark Gertler — Selected Letters*, edited by Noel Carrington (Rupert Hart-Davis, 1965)

Mountains

Mountains

Looking up (say a year old, sixteen months)
she was a glacier forty foot high
white-print flowers on her pinafore
edelweiss across a mountain-side,
her voice coming from the summit down to me.
My ice-pick fingers couldn't get a grip.

I wanted whatever I could hang on to:
a shin, a wrist, an avalanche,
where her heavy arms loosened like snow
and I was lifted to the crevice between neck and shoulder
on a level with her eyes.

At sixteen months
my daughter's at my feet: far down there,
her cries grapple-hooks pinning their hopes.
Any minute she'll climb inside me.
I want to be ice. She can't move mountains.
The season's shifting. I want to give way.

The Man and the Dog

When my father went out
saying he was going
to see a man about a dog
I saw the dog.

Perhaps an alsatian this time,
dragging him home on its long chain
gagging at its tight spiked collar.
The dog never came.

One evening my father went out
without saying where.
I sat like my mother
waiting for his key in the lock.

She was the man of the house now
whether or not she wanted to be.
I thought if he won't come back
I'll untie the dog to sniff him out for me.

There was no dog. No man.
Years after he left
I found out he wasn't my father.

Duet

My mother and Ella Fitzgerald sing
a duet. This memory out of nowhere.
She's got time for the radio. It's Sunday morning.
While she irons another sleeve or collar
her voice dips and lifts below Ella's effortless
skylark. It's *Moonlight in Vermont:* a place
she's never seen, though she lulls each note with her guess
at beauty. Clarinet and strings, that grace
and longing behind their harmony. I play with panthers
and zebras across the carpet. What are these women
teaching me by their tune? Maybe stars
belong to lovers, even
if they never catch them. Maybe someone
stole their moonlight, so they sing for its return.

Mother's Son

I'll wake you early.
We'll walk to the swans, your favourite lake.
You can laugh again at pigeons
clapping higher than our shoulders
when we step onto their breadcrumbs in the sun.
While we sit inside a café cupping tea,
squint through glass at the steepling fountain
you can laugh at your black forest gateau.
We're on a jaunt again, a spree, and you
as you always were, determined to make the most of it:
eavesdrop on other customers, share a joke,
laugh yourself silly when the wind
whips up your skirt on the promenade.
Remember? Can you?

You and your sisters
at a family ritual, our Boxing Day parties,
singing *Boogie Woogie Bugle Boy*
miming trumpets, half-cut on babycham.
Yanking my hand to Infants that first morning,
me gripping radiators and doorjambs
while everyone gawped. "If you don't behave
I'll take you home." *Yes take me home
please take me home.*
Once when I went too far
you smashed a milk bottle into my hair.
A glass triangle sank in my forearm.
I told the nurse I fell. She sewed four stitches.
"Don't ask me to remember."

Clearing your flat
we nab a wedding photo:
you step from the car in your silver sandal,
a young dark Ingrid Bergman
veiled, your girl's face blurred and waiting
to be given away, for him to lift the veil.
You're unfinished, changing as smoke:
a foggy view now with no-one to lift it.
At the home where they call you *strong as a lion*
there's a wall of familiar photos in your room.
Touching your grandchildren's faces
like holy relics, saying "Lovely. Lovely."
Taking my hand
when we walk the corridor saying "Allright Dad."

Helping Her Stand

I help my mother get up from a chair
by grabbing both hands and pulling,
straining her weight against mine. Her
slippers slap the carpet, as if we're fooling
around while I ask for the last dance.
We giggle. I grip and heave. Her panicky foothold
drags on solid ground, because once
she believes I can raise her, she would
feel I'm stronger now. She, who I leant on
like pressing my forehead against warm rock,
might let herself be lifted by her son
into his arms. Her fear of falling could break
against my chest. Of course I can hold her.
We sway with our success. I kiss her hair.

Looking for the Square

Where there should be a road there's a river,
where I remember a courtyard
we cross the fifth bridge.
We're following our noses
to a dead end (wall) a dead end (water).
We want that square with its dry fountain
and a café with tables outside,
where couples toast each other's arrival:
candles in waxy bottles, chilled wine.

I'm sure we came this way earlier
although the sky has changed.
Old women lean from long windows
opening their arms to pull the shutters closed.
Shops go dark. It's time for lights.
Now we're a couple rowing about directions,
while passers-by avert their eyes or gawp.
I sulk beside you like a bad dog for three street-corners.

We dawdle past dim shop windows.
Here's one full of hard bread,
another with marbled boxes and beaky masks.
Because we stop looking we find that square
under its own half-moon.
Some couples stare at each other's eyes
by candlelight, as expected,
while these pass photos of their children
backwards and forwards over the tablecloth.
A few sit alone, toasting the chair opposite.
The waiters know by our clothes we can't afford it.
We back off, take a breather instead, and keep walking.

A Land That May

She said "Talk.
I do all the talking. Tell me what *you* feel."

Beware, this field is mined:
a word that means one word to you
a safe footing, careful step,
can blow up in your face.
Take the quick word fear:
I fear that you —
"You fear that I? Fear. What have you to fear
after all I've done shown been?"
See what I mean.
Even if you beware
of quicksands, covered traps,
pits innocent as a mesh of sunburnt leaves
under your feet
what choice do you have?
Silence, yes but silence
hides its own quicksands traps and pits
dug behind shut lips.
The only way forward is forward,
knowing one word like fear or love's a hand-grenade
lobbed back and forth from barricades
either side of this punctured field.
No man's land, no woman's land:
a land that may
with talk, with turning each word over
reverently as if handling eggshells,
a land that may sprout aconites next year.

Driving Through Fog

In a car built for breakdown any moment
dipped beams part the waves,
sleepwalk into smoggy roses
serrated by half-open shears of light.

Tonight I know these black backroads by heart:
each hump and ditch, each narrow mile.
It's tunnel vision, feel the way
trusting that I'm bound for, bound to, you.

Last Night and Tonight

Why can we kiss
when words coming out of our mouths
last night were meant to cut
as if we chewed and spat glass?

These are the same mouths:
our tongues licking side teeth now
the roof and the throat's wet cove,
words not hard anymore
quiet, blending like one hand stroking each finger
to its tip, tiny pyramids of knuckles now
the palm, another hand.

I'm open as a woman tonight
take whatever you want
hard as a man I'll give myself
and take from you, this rhythm, this give and take.

A Starling in the Top Room

I haven't been up here for days. There's bird-shit
on the typewriter: dried mud and white
spat all over my papers. On the carpet
between the chair-legs it's laid out
like an offering: the speckled breast,
tail-feathers a shut black fan
spindly claws limp as a snapped wrist.
There's green on the wing when it rolls in the dustpan.
Christ knows how it got here. I won't let the kids touch
in case it wakes up and pecks out their eyes.
What am I scared of? That panicky screech
round my room, the skull hitting glass when it flies,
as if it's inside an egg held up to
the light, and it can't smash through.

Lady Falls
(Pont-Nedd-Fechan)

She's falling through an endless backward dive
over the lip:
a glinty roll of film winding fast
into brown water.

I'm behind her
feeling spat at and immune.
I'm no stone
prepared to bear her white rain forever.

When I look up
the pour is drumming uphill now,
unreeling with me into cloud
as if she'll promise soft hair down my shoulders.

If I step under
will she plaster these clothes to my skin,
leave me gagging for air
steeped as a wrist in cold fire?

Waiting for Water-Lilies

It's the wrong season.
Pads are strung to the moorings
without those sunbathed petals
bobbing their paper yachts
like the ones you tried to paint before you died.

You gave up painting lilies. Now I remember,
started aiming for reflections:
how each pad weighed on the surface
as if hovering over clouds sculling above it
through railings of light and drizzle,
three fat fish between wobbling trees.

It takes ages to notice the frogs:
the colour and size of stones
on the pond's dusky floor.
Small males pinned like brooches
to the backs of big-mother females.

I want to show you that pair under a pad:
her belly the swollen underside of an ivy-leaf,
still flippers splayed
her throat stashed in moss,
the mate tight as a fist
not letting go
as if the act of holding on can make her alive.

The Need

To be released from the need for her, always hungry,
rising apart from each other now
like two stars this evening:
the space between
precious as any glow we offer.

Once I assumed her skin was mine
I could suckle and burrow like a child
and her the mother. How wrong can you get.
She wants a man or none at all:
one child more would weigh her down
until she sinks in the river.

If I could imagine
a place for love without needing her
I'd rise like Adam from the valley in her side,
stepping out from the home of her skin
into mine.

Our Stories

Each word used like a knife on fire
to burn ourselves or prise apart a clam
eating its mess inside.

What are our stories? Tell them.
About bridges to meet broken fathers,
about how the ones we love looked
when breath emptied their mouths.
Now we're lifting sleepy children onto shoulders
or mourning those we couldn't have.

When we start our stories this evening
there's no way to stop.
We become bores – pissed on words – an embarrassment.
Stragglers who gather to listen
chuck money to shut us up
and run for home.

If I speak for myself
it worms a way through where harebells
buffet above the sea
a way to find words if it kills me,
to apologise for overstating
and overstate again,
called away from ending the story
by my crying child.

Die
Bravely

Why this would make a man a man of salt,
To use his eyes for garden water-pots,
Ay, and laying autumn's dust. I will die bravely,
Like a smug bridegroom.

King Lear (Act 4 Scene 6)

Morning After

Last night we threw all the junk overboard:
chucked out summer photos and simple promises,
their noise fat stones hitting water.
Last night we climbed into our life-rafts
like separate beds.

This morning
the marriage is floating away from us.

If we stretch we can still touch its rudder,
its soaked wood.
Our hands are full enough, steadying ourselves in the wake
where there's no sound of gulls, no sight of land,
only sea growing flatter between us in a new light.

Your First Words

"Can I say hello to you?" We were eighteen
first night away from home, and I said yes.
You thought I looked safe. How could you guess
in years to come I'd sometimes leave the room when
you were talking, annul you like that, how often
I'd stone you with silence. If I managed to impress
that night with quotes from Plath it didn't take us
long to learn no-one lives by poetry alone.
Pillow-talk on student grants. Two virgins touching
skin and histories. Speech ran
its thread down boulevards and cul-de-sacs, finding
all there is to know about one person.
Twenty years on I barely know you, but thanks for asking.
Go back to that night and I'd say yes again.

Separation Suite

They sit a chair apart,
move when the counsellor calls them
to a room where they're meant to relate.

Three fawn chairs and they talk about needs.
She's only starting to imagine hers,
can't begin to name them. He's written a list.

Next week he's back without her.
One voice slumped against magnolia woodchip:
his pain aria, his monotonous solo.

Looking at Wedding Photos

Who are these kids dressed as adults, thinking
they can throw a promise at the future
and it won't shatter after sixteen years? They're
sticking a knife in the cake hand over hand, grinning
fit to burst. Remember that Just Married sign
felt-tipped on the back of a Rat Poison container,
your dad getting lost, yellow roses, our
first married row on the wedding
night round Salisbury's one-way system. All gone.
What happened next? Happiness. Mistakes. Slowly seeing we've
got to cut our losses. I won't burn
these smiles. They're proof of love,
while our children who never existed then
hold out their gifts: three reasons to survive.

The Old Words

While my hands soak up to their wrists in water
and the kids breathe asleep upstairs
my head's a hive with you and him naked in it.

Funny how the old words come back.
Fuck. Adultery. Cuckold. Betrayal.

I want this porn-film out of my hair:
to wash off what your body's doing, not doing
your skin a map I can no longer follow,
whetstone where a new knife twists.

Ivy House

A couple of dreamers. We'd make our ideal home.
So what if the owners were splitting up?
We were rock solid, seduced by each snowdrop
daffodil and door-frame, the view from every room.
We put down roots: damp-proofed, re-wired, sprayed
                                                 woodworm,
coated on buckets of gloss. We couldn't stop
until french windows had their cat-flap
and kids' hand-marks swiped the walls. It was high time
to look at what we'd done. I stayed tense
as barbed wire while you started scratching
a tunnel out. The builder said subsidence:
that quarter-inch crack down the north wall. Re-pointing
can't cure it. A fine romance.
It'll cost an arm and a leg now the drains are collapsing.

From Under the Shadow

Don't kid yourself it's easy.
My shadow's not as vacuous as air,
some sticky web wiped from footsoles.
It's heavy as a man's body on you
squeezing out your breath.

We pressed grids across each other,
tattooing a street-plan of bruises
under our skin: husband father wife mother.
Live in my image. We couldn't fit.

Rip the maps,
learn our names again, recognize for the first time
your face, my face at noon where nettle paths divide
and our shadows shrink to puddles we step over.

Slow Learner

I keep rehearsing the call you won't make
one night near midnight in a few months: "I was wrong.
He's nothing to me. I've loved you all along.
I see things now. I made a mistake.
We both did, but we've learnt from it. If we take
our time maybe we could look at starting again." This daft song
round my skull, these phrases that don't belong
in your mouth but in mine, or that fake
image I still have of you. I never could see
what was an inch from my nose. It's like two days
before Clifford died, when they'd already
upped the morphine, his doctor friend says
"You know he's dying don't you?" I thought he can't be.
He'll recover. Pinning my hopes on another bad phase.

Talk Before Bedtime

Our son touches his forehead
runs a hand down his body to his feet:
"I felt sad from here to here."

We talk about sadness
how you and I can't make each other happy.

Squeezing my ribs in his tightest bear-hug
he laughs and asks "Does that hurt?"

In Front of the Kids

When I cried in front of the kids they asked why.
"I've made you unhappy." That was enough.
I didn't add no-one would choose this rough
ride for their children, how I followed my
father's footsteps by walking out. That advert family
drops through the floorboards. I won't bluff
my way through failing as husband or father. My tough
son ran for toilet-paper to dry
my eyes. He said "I want to see you"
and gently held my face between his hands.
If this home's broken we'll build something new
from the four times a week when I'm with them,
                                        stroking strands
of hair off their hot brows. We slip through
absences, over stones, and our river never ends.

Benediction

Bless you for entering through a door-crack
and opening windows. For three children.
Without them my life would be one room,
books and a bare lightbulb, a locked cupboard.

For knowing when we needed to end:
saving us years of petty victories
over dinner, on a drive, our children
watching and hearing, a gagged audience.

For handing me back to myself:
giving up your responsibility, saying
"He's yours now. Make of his life what you can."

Truce

Call a truce. I'll bite my tongue and remember
how your breath fanned my back while we slept.
If it tickled my skin I shifted, slipped
an arm around your waist sometimes, or under
the duvet on good nights you squeezed my shoulder.
No need for talking in our sleep. Our bodies kept
their independent language, whose tides swept
us up pebbles and rolled us down. Until the past year
made us kneel yards apart on a hard coast.
Six weeks after we faced that truth
it was almost the old days. You dozed on my chest
as if you were my wife again, my breath
against your hair. Letting go. The last time we kissed
I lightly nipped your tongue between my teeth.

Her Voice

I haven't walked far enough. I can still hear it:
her words repeat in my head
until they're mine.

Hedges creak in the wind like bed-springs.
Her voice will go the way of rain:
shrink to a shallowing puddle, dry in the sun.

I can sit it out
while that noise from one skylark in the next field
flickers its singed coal above my breathing.

The
Wolf's
Tale

The Wolf's Tale

The kids are back with mum
nuzzling her bagpipe udders again,
and wolf has paid his dues
belly full of stones at the bottom of the well.

Before his muzzle bubbles under water
what if a woman, the woodcutter's daughter,
walks down to the well?
What if she pities a drowning wolf,
pulls him up in her bucket
like a great soggy prize
while he howls his tale of woe,
how these kids cut his belly wide open
packed it with stones?

This woman snips mummy-goat's cross-stitch
until he's open again to the sun,
ribs stacked like a drystone wall.
One by one she unloads his stones
saying "Trust me. Trust me."
Watch the wolf.
With each stone gone he's a gaping suitcase.
As fast as she hauls them out
he piles them back, scared of being empty.

This woman's no fool.
She takes her pail of water through the woods
and is never seen again.
He's still undone. That hole's as big as he is.
Can he give up the notion of filling it with bricks or kids?
Look. He sews himself up,
leaves a space for his organs to breathe
for his blood to twist through its circuits,
leaves his ribcage room for its wolfish heart.

Night Drive into Snow

Rice-grains chucked in his face. Their pellets won't sting.
He's dumped here, a thick bridegroom
white knuckling the wheel.

It's television interference. A million goose-quills shot at
his head:
a pincushion any minute
if he's lulled into counting ticks lit by the beam.
Ice locusts eat his windscreen easy as skin-leaf.

If he once forgets to aim
for that shiny half-mile mapped ahead
he's finished.

Room Key

Run this key-ring like a fish
through your fingers.
Slip the key into its lock
worn along the grooves like rubbed brass.

Of course every wall's magnolia. But look:
you can arrange a set of postcards
on this wardrobe. Backs of women in church,
a glass of flowers, a tree in bloom.

If there's a sound like a mouse-scratch
ignore it.

There are four rooms like this in the building.
Four men live here without women.
Each man has his own soap and razor, his own toilet-roll.
Some men stay here for years.

The fish key-ring tickles your palm.
Its joints bend and click like it's swimming.
You're a slippery customer.
Take it. It's yours.

Deciding Who Gets What

Don't give your new lover the rocking chair.
For him it'll be another place to sway
while he does whatever he does. He won't know,
unless you tell him, I bought it for you
after our first child: bought this image
of you feeding your milky mother-love
but the milk wouldn't come. I rocked
each broken night, not knowing his cries were dry hunger,
until the health visitor weighed him and warned
he was fading away. We used it less
with our next child, hardly touched it with the last:
that icon for a life ticking forward and backward,
moving and stuck, admitting this has to change.

Absent Parent

1. Down the Aisles

When I watch fathers now my envy
echoes those months before our first child
while I studied their strokes and kisses, every
gesture a dumb password to that proud
exhausted brotherhood. See how simply this one
lifts his kicking daughter into the trolley
like she's six bags of demerara, a box of wine.
That far back I was ready
as plums to cram fatherhood's mouth,
glut myself with babies. Now I'm empty
I could warn the others in a breath:
Look at me —
no child at my side, one of those fathers
hungry for the moment when my cheek rests on theirs.

2. This House

If you ask years later "Why did you,
why didn't you?" I could say
how leaving your mother meant leaving you
and when I dived in that river
I didn't know where I'd surface.
How your toothbrushes hang in my bathroom,
your sandles unbuckled by the bed.
How I drive six motorways to see you
and in the gaps between weekends and phonecalls
this house wants your bikes
scuffing its wallpaper, your legs
tangling its sheets.
How I hope as my dad hoped of me
you'll end up at my door.

3. *Wave Machine*

Sirens and lights introduce it, hook us in.
We're a wet crowd paying dry money to be rocked
today by artificial tides. Your brothers begin
a slow sway down the deep end, while we're knocked
and doused in the shallows. You scoop water
in armfuls over you, sluice your skin with a belly-dive
wild as instinct. Jump the waves, my wringing daughter.
When one floods your mouth I pat your back. I must drive
you home tomorrow: your place, not mine.
You'll make me count how many days until
you see me, using my fingers and yours to reach thirteen.
Dance for every minute that matters: when we roll
or bump together now, rinsed as pebbles over
and over, and you sing in my ear.

Into Snow
for Ian Jones

You're walking away from everyone into snow:
voices of those you love can't drag you back,
the syllables of your name a cracked bell
tongued in your ear.

You're leaving the pen and ink leaf-shadow,
hills a white nothing where you're one man
squashing the depth of boot-soles into drifts,
breath the only heat to keep you alive.

As if it quietly answers instinct
your body admits it's time to rest:
you want a sleeping-bag, a pillow for your head.

You're lying down and making wounds
as if you choose to die in battle,
your last night under the miles between stars.

A Tree in the Wood

'A Conservative councillor committed suicide the day he was due to appear in court charged with cottaging offences. He was found hanging from a tree. The 40-year-old father of two was due to appear following his arrest for gross indecency at public toilets in Leeds. As well as hanging himself he had also slashed both his wrists.'
'Gay Times'

Once we make contact,
our skin matches struck against each other
I stick to my rule never to kiss.
Lick and suck and gag on it sometimes
without wet kisses, little or less eye to eye,
ramming two fingers like a gun inside his hole.

It's not love, this function, this need
to paw and squeeze, pull back his foreskin,
get out afterwards quick as a wank, wipe myself clean.
I love the wife I kiss in bed at night. Our pearly daughters.
In our cottage where armchairs match the curtains
I smell this other cottage, its men and hand-jobs,
dates and sizes felt-tipped on the tiles.

If it's love I must be cut in two:
stop the body to stop its feelings.
If this sense floods my skin for minutes,
eating a man hungry into my mouth
swallowing swords, kneading his inches,
feeling good alive together in our sweat
my neck must need rope's love-bites,
my wrists loosening their grip as he shoots
deserve these slits. My blood can wipe me clean.

Sisters

We became the Beverley Sisters at break.
Three mummy's-boy first years in an all boys school,
standing out like cockatoos at a wake.
What drew us together? We weren't cool
in that sad male way we envied and watched
as we half-hid past the toilets, near
the fire escape. It'd be a botched
job if we aimed to be men one day. Much better
to be sisters. What harmony! *There were never
such devoted sisters.* No stilettos, no
sequins, no blonde wigs then. *I've got my eye on her.*
We sashayed and fingerclicked thirty years ago.
Months before you died we met in London again:
you two gay, me halfway there. Brothers under the skin.

Queer

How old was I? Thirteen maybe.
One insult too many smashed that armour
I'd constructed: "Fucking queer."
This classmate looked inside me,
knew the secret, smelt it. What made him see?
Me fancying men, other boys. Watching their
legs inside jeans, their chests under
buttoned shirts, a throat or a knee.
I sniffed it with him:
disgust; difference; always outside; never let in
to marriage, kids, happiness. Locked in that bathroom
for an hour, thinking: *Take it away. I'll pull off my skin,
stop my eyes, do anything. I'm not one of them.*
How long does it take to own yourself? How long has it been?

The Coming Out Group

He said "We've always been honest
so I told my wife I'm gay. Five minutes later
she was throwing my clothes out the window.
I've not seen my kids for a month.
When I told my mum she said
'You can still visit but don't bring
your poofy friends here.'
At work they wrote queer on my windscreen.
I've lost everything but it's worth it.
I'm true to myself", and he punched his chest
once, hard.

Pink Triangle

You think I'm unspeakable? Hear me,
my name spat at enough to be forgotten
like smoke through cloud.

Wash me whenever the rain leaks.
Crackle my sweat in sun:
the same I lazed under months ago,
dreaming none could judge or hope to touch me.

I belong to open windows, wine on a kiss.
Our masters decided otherwise:
condemned to difference when difference is death.
If I'm shunned it's a bitter home.

Home? Outcast even here,
this pink the only flag I need to honour.
Black bread. This skin a shipwreck,
my first resistance a promise to survive.

Of course I'm frightened,
snapping lice in my fingers,
my second resistance
noticing his eyes.

On the Bed

On the bed with you, shoes and jackets off
after my first date in twenty years,
half a minute before a kiss, I couldn't tell
what netting a man might answer.

We're unbuttoning buttons:
nipples, unfamiliar shoulders, forearms and fingers
dance the body's yes
feed me I want I'll give tongued in each kiss.

Sense of Skin

feeling it like a breath
on mine,
the exact sense of his skin.
John Sewell
(from *Black Waterfall*)

Each man, when he enters
wondering if he's welcome in the half-light
if your skin will work for him,
each man enters a quiet minute
to look at each other's eyes before you begin.

Darkness snuffs a blur along hard edges
where fingers now, slow fingers, trace a subtle inch
across another skin, this naked land.
Feel difference: his difference, yours,
the chest-hairs tickle or smooth,
shoulders learning to yield again,
the cock that fits the hand,
inside the wet magenta comfort of a mouth
and sometimes (if you sense
he won't) the slightest slip of kiss
to a turned nape or warm ring in the lobe,
sweat-glimmer on his forehead, perhaps a tongue.

Bodies become miraculous: this moment of conspiracy,
palm to belly, balls to lips.
This, that is degraded, proclaims its place, its riches
beside the throat of any iris swallowing dark.
As much a right, as wondrous, as a hand
discovering the length of his unlocked arm
meets another hand to clench it,
link it briefly and let go.

Revolution

We led a revolution in each other.
For you the simple fact that someone
loves you has smashed windows, broken
the locks, blown open your banks, churches, your
courts. We untie the blindfold, take that prisoner
by the hand to a secluded garden
where the magnolia spills its teacups one by one.
When signs say keep off we lounge on clover
and when we kiss no-one watching turns a hair.
My revolution's loving another man.
While crowds run through streets, and we're footsore
after the marches, dry from singing, we can
open our door, climb this shaky stair
and swim inside each other's arms again.

The Rule of Earth

The rule
of earth is attachment:

here what can't be held
is.

Mark Doty
(from *The Wings*)

Two Men Together

When our next-door neighbour asked "Have you ever
been married?" you wanted to say "I am now,"
but decided to answer "No, never"
to suit you both: spare her blushes, allow
discretion in place of honesty. Tonight
undressing for bed you tell this story
and I ask you to bite your tongue about
our life, two men together. Are we cowards choosing safety
in a bolt-hole? Knowing each neighbour
might already guess, but never would say. Knowing
the cost of avoiding kisses before
the bay window. We're going
down under the duvet. If we touch
with the lights on for hours no-one can watch.

The Night Before

Our opening night. Three hours after that first drink
I asked you back to my room. I noticed the moon
smudge my window while two panting men
fandango'd on the sheet. Our white ink
spilt on linen before we sank
to sleep. Did anything else happen
as we dreamed? Unfamiliar elbows, nudging skin:
one night stand in a hot bed, on the brink
of an awkward morning. The colour changed, lit
from inside like a new world
where we could find no language yet,
because we hadn't spoken it. When you smiled
across the pillow through that first light
I fell in love, dumbly, like a wondering child.

Each Other's Skin

What animals we are! Dipping to feed
off each other's skin, lick each other dry.
Such hunger can only be glutted by
the giving and taking of touch, like our greed
for air or water, slaking the belly. This need
to feel snared by your arms the minute I
squeeze you in mine, while we both lie
caught, triumphant, forgetting to be freed.
Quiver inside my mouth again, each splash
salt to the throat, smeared on me rolling
under and over. My body's lost where I finish,
where you begin. Fingers dapple me, stroking.
Bite my kisses and kiss them better. Unleash
the tongue to its work, the cock to its crowing.

Test

A few months after we met we took the test.
This badge of commitment: button plasters
in the crooks of our arms; waiting eight hours
for a nurse to call us negative. That chaste
word lit our lucky blood, handing us the rest
of our years to waltz by disasters
like this one, as if our stars
struck gold and would again. You swayed on my chest
under moonlight, where we nearly felt safe.
It hadn't slipped through your arteries
down my gulleys and cul-de-sacs, its grief
nibbling your ear-lobes, stroking my sleeves.
It let us imagine a future instead, our life
the colour of water when a shadow leaves.

Five Years After

We were both very young and probably unsuited.
And it is over now and nobody's fault.
Mark Gertler to Carrington, March 1932

Five years after she and I parted
we walk into their garden, where she sits
beside him, calm as sunlight. His hand fits
into hers, and they're chatting. We've interrupted
to say we're off home, honey colour slanted
through branches onto our heads. Our daughter skips
between grown-ups calling for a goodbye kiss.
We leave them to their new home, as if we've granted
each other a blessing, another chance:
regret and anger trickling into grass,
or away into weather we all moved under once.
Next morning you bend to press
seed-potatoes into the vegetable patch. I balance
to paint our hall like a big yellow yes.

Luck or Judgement

If I half-wake at night and touch you
we brush past each other in our dreams:
knock a wrist, bump a shoulder. It seems
however apart we've been, our bodies know
sleeping together makes each day worth walking through.
This gentle collision into each other's arms,
that hushed answer spoken by the dark, brims
me over again like wax spilt from a candle.
We're linked for however long it lasts,
this luck or judgement, your breath on mine.
If it's been a slow moon rising, no-one asks
for promises, a window free of rain.
It's enough to draw the curtains, quieten our ghosts
with a kiss tonight, be alone.

Bluebells

Follow me inside the hidden wood,
taking us both down a narrow path
printed by boot-soles. This haven holds our breath.
Smoky pagodas cluster: a low mauve cloud
where sun-leaves shiver the hide
of blue tigers, moving through undergrowth.
They'll sleep in a minute, a shadow's tablecloth
settled over their haunches. We could
eat here. We could drink the dusky scent
that lingers every year, committed to coming back
to this place. Thinking about commitment,
people we miss and meet again, others we lack,
I lean towards you like a tree that's leant
the way the wind blows, learning not to break.

Lover's Knot

Sometimes this need swarms out of my skin
to nest in you. Is it simply desire?
As if touching home and warm must appear
outside the self, to be met this time in
you. It's a knot I can't untwist alone,
expecting you to be my Alexander
unsheathing your sword to slice through fire,
undo and conquer me. Did I plan
to hand over the keys so easily?
Not this time. I'd rather unpick the strings
spooling my ribs and wrists myself, see
you untie your own these rainy evenings.
Salving ourselves as if, by loosening bandages, we
might begin to unwrap each other's wings.

Diagnosis

From the foot of your hospital bed the doctor
described your heart: its infection, its leaky valve,
surgery in a few months to solve
the problem. We needed some air
and discovered a garden with a slow fan of water
drowning geraniums. You said "How instructive
this is!" We kept quiet a while to give
ourselves a breather, next year
already mapped out for us: a line
of stitches down your chest, taking it easy,
a slow recovery. Is this the heart's infection,
this need to keep less than a beat away
from each other whatever might happen?
I watched wet leaves. You watched the water sway.

Two Birds

Alone in our garden, where you should be,
I keep remembering that crow
hanging above my head a few weeks ago:
a croaky omen I couldn't shake away
bearing some dark message about destiny.
Most likely those dogged caws were meant to throw
me off the scent of a kill, protect its young. We borrow
easy explanations, knowing I rob too many
metaphors from birds, foxes, weather.
While I think of you now on the ward, thin
and asking no questions, there's a clapped stir
on the rooftop, where a ringdove settles to win
me over with its calm. You're a born survivor
if the ringdove's home to roost and the crow's gone.

The Surgeon's Talk

I expect to notice his hands, how his fingers
could balance your heart like an egg
with its chick jiggling inside. He won't brag
about his knowledge. Knowing we've no answers
he forgives our fear and checks your papers,
test-results, helps us touch the big
unknown hole of your operation. He's got to jog
us with that subtle word mortality, take us
to its edge, show the high success rate,
soothe us with his voice while we both look over.
The odds are good. We might
even trust them. He shakes hands from the other
side of health, and we're back in the bright
waiting-room wanting a stiff drink to recover.

The Thought

If I lose you. Watch how I bear the thought:
if I lose you. Never to sense again
your palm against my face while we explain
the way this day has gone, each night
across the pillows, talking late
with kisses when we could have slept. To remain
in a wood shouting your name among trees when
there's no more chance of an answer. What
am I doing rehearsing the life I fear most?
Stay a little longer. You help to hold at bay
the emptiness under everything, just
your hand can achieve that, yes, against my
skin. The pressure of your fingers can insist
this is what matters: us. Here. Today.

Inside the Ring

We laze on grass at the festival,
tapping toes and fingers for the beat.
Kissing's easy here: a space to meet
other outsiders, who touch and loll
across each other as if that's all
they need to do; imagining the right
to act this freely down whatever street
we choose, as if it's natural.
Later, leaving the crowd, we step into a circle
of toadstools, their fawn thumbs a ring for fairies.
We kiss inside it, quick and happy, the ripple
of evening music yards away. The diva cries.
We're walking outside safety now, this simple
touch enough to change our lives.

Before

One week before your operation
you've become glass to me:
a delicate vessel holding all you might be
between unsteady hands. This motion
of crossing a room could tip your libation.
I wait in the kitchen, not wanting to miss any
drop of you walking towards me. I see
pyjamas in a half-packed suitcase open
upstairs. I'm a father letting you go
for a ride with strangers, out of my sight.
Treat him well, I want to say. You don't know
his gifts: how memorable the light
has become since he stood by this window;
his breath stroking my spine in bed last night.

Post-Op

They opened your skin to its frailty,
shut you, sent you back changed. You've landed
propped on pillows after a deep-sea dive: winded,
wired up, the air pipe playing its flutey
whistle through your teeth, your glassy
stare half-lidded. You're out of it. I'm stranded
on the sidelines, dry-eyed, dumbfounded,
reading a ward sign: *After heart surgery*
your heart needs to return to its normal state
of balance. I watch your chest with dread:
its surge and dip, its flicker the only sight
I understand, while others wait by each lit bed.
Love dragged us under, where we sit
softly calling our living back from the dead.

Your Voice

Your voice knows the rhythm to calm me.
If I phone from work and hear you it takes
me home. Away from being this man who makes
decisions. Back to where it's quiet and I see
your eyes. In the kitchen one morning we
clear up kids' bowls of half-eaten cornflakes,
half-drunk drinks, and your voice shakes:
"I love you so much I can't tell you. They
ain't made the words." Each phrase transforms
me into a man who'll throw away his fear
like crumbs to sparrows, walk through rooms
sometimes to hear you sing, press his ear
to your voice on the ansaphone: saying our names
in the same breath; promising we're not here.

Miles Away

You're under glass again, inside silence.
When you shut up
I'm shut out from wherever you slip
your thoughts: paper boats blown in soft defiance
to another shore. I nag myself: *no self-reliance;*
too cloying; let him be. I drain your emptied cup
as if it's mine, expecting to lick the last drop.
Allow his right to silence, his space, his difference.
The deficit is mine. Having chosen
you in all your sun and shade, your words and your
quiet, how can I say I want one leaf broken
from your stem, changing who you are?
If you feel absent then, this loss unspoken,
I only need to let you say "I'm here."

A Lazy Minute

I spend a lazy minute looking at my hand
folded like a small wing on your shoulder.
As you doze I notice I'm getting older:
tiny cracked ice lattice-work scanned
over my skin, my country's web pinned
across this body to light the continuous border
between me and you. I'm goose-pimpled, feeling colder,
while you pull me towards the sound
of easy breathing. I see a single
wild arabesque of hair near your vaccination-scar.
We're as different as our bodies, yet mingle
legs under the duvet as if we'd blur
ourselves together if we could: shingle
and sea, sycamore and cypress, flint and fire.

Seeing My Mother

My love grew another leaf when you said
seeing my mother teaches you something
about being alive. Others say there's nothing
left now her mind's gone. She'd be better off dead.
You see her simplified need
to sit with her fingers touching
mine for family news, the old stories, laughing
at whatever memory we might have freed.
All we have to do is stay there
talking, listening as her word-noises
and made-up half tunes lilt on air,
like she's humming to herself while a tide washes
round her shins, rising higher,
her happy song drowning the sea's voices.

Tunnel of Leaves

Driving to meet the children by the sea
we enter a tunnel of leaves. Sunlight
dabbles the windscreen, our sight
dazed, squinted, assuming we can see
the same dazzle. Striped by shadows, you beside me,
becoming the music we're hearing: this flight
of wings a waterfall, green over white
on our upturned faces. We barely
remember where we're heading. Only
that we're driving to meet them, speeding
through minutes, trees or tarmac, nearly
forgetting which: asking the wrong thing
if we want this to stand still, its beauty
being always in the moving.

Walking Together

I'm learning to slow my steps in time with yours.
There's seventeen years between us: a gap
I called a challenge once, the way love ignores
any barrier, mountain, distance. I'd stop
a minute to let you catch up in those early days.
Carried away by how often we said
"Let's go for it" when we met, I read that phrase
as my green light, the same light we saw ahead
walking back last night to our posh hotel.
It glowed at the crest of an avenue of trees
still young and green, while a heart-shadow fell
at our feet from a streetlamp through leaves.
We paused, and in that gap I took your arm
for a few yards of dark, with miles to get home.

Biographical Notes

Robert Hamberger was born in 1957 in Whitechapel, London. In 1985 he was awarded a Writer's Bursary by East Midlands Arts. His poetry has been broadcast on Radio 4 and he has taken part in numerous poetry readings in London and the East Midlands. He has published five pamphlet selections: *No Green Leaves* (1979), *The Tunes of Risky Weather* (1985), *Journey to a Birth* (1987) *The Wolf's Tale* (1995) and *The Rule of Earth* (2001). Robert Hamberger's poems have appeared in various anthologies, including Faber & Faber's *Hard Lines 2* and A&C Black's *Sing For Your Life,* an anthology for schools. In 1995 he was awarded a Hawthornden Fellowship. In 1997 his first full-length collection *Warpaint Angel* was published by Blackwater Press.

Also Available from Five Leaves

Passionate Renewal: Jewish poetry in Britain since 1945. An anthology edited by *Peter Lawson*
354 pages, 0 907123 73 2, £14.99
A Poetry Book Society Special Commendation

Dannie Abse **Richard Burns** Ruth Fainlight **Elaine Feinstein** Karen Gershon **Michael Hamburger** Philip Hobsbaum **Michael Horovitz** A.C. Jacobs **Bernard Kops** Lotte Kramer **Joanne Limburg** Emanuel Litvinoff **Gerda Mayer** Jeremy Robson **Michael Rosen** Jon Silkin **George Szirtes** Jonathan Treitel **Daniel Weissbort**
The act of gathering these (poets) together reveals the importance of Jewish writers to a wider British tradition, both as poets, but also as translators, and communicators with the wider world. This is an important and revealing anthology.
Poetry Book Society

The Art of Blessing the Day: Poems on Jewish Themes by *Marge Piercy*
0 907123 47 3, 200 pages, £7.99
A collection based on themes of family (*mishpocheh*), repair of the world (*tikkun olam*), history and interpretation (*toladot, midrashim*), prayer (*tefillah*) and the Jewish year (*ha-shana*).
This is what I want from poetry: generosity, sensuous imagery, musicality, celebration, the voice of community.
Poetry Quarterly Review

Gardens of Eden Revisited by *Michelene Wandor*
0 907123 62 7, 186 pages, £7.99
...a gossipy irresistible send-up of the Old Testament.
Vogue

The Radical Twenties: Writing, Politics, Culture
by *John Lucas*
0 907123 17 1, 263 pages, £11.99
What is particularly valuable in this book is the attention Lucas gives to a number of texts from the 1920s that have had less attention than they deserve in literary-critical accounts of the decade... the dust-jacket photograph of Nan Youngman in 1925 with cigarette and guitar, so wonderfully evocative of the spirit Lucas respects and consistently carries forward in his writing.
MLR

This is No Book: A Gay Reader by *Gregory Woods*
0 907123 26 0, 112 pages, £6.95

...a marvellous read - witty and independent and full of shrewd insights from, I suppose, the foremost gay poet working in Britain today. If you want to map out a gay canon, start here: a colleague asked me what had been done on gay poetics and I can't think of anything better. Gay Times

Poems for the Beekeeper edited by *Robert Gent*
0 907123 82 1, 200 pages, £6.99

Dannie Abse **Fleur Adcock** James Berry **Alan Brownjohn** Catheryn Byron **Wendy Cope** Robert Creeley **Kwame Dawes** Carol Anne Duffy **Helen Dunmore** Gavin Ewart **UA Fanthorpe** Elaine Feinstein **John Harvey** Adrian Henri **Selima Hill** Mick Imlah **Jenny Joseph** Jackie Kay **Liz Lochhead** Michael Longley **John Lucas** Roger McGough **Ian McMillan** Wes Magee **Adrian Mitchell** Henry Normal **Brian Patten** Tom Paulin **Nigel Planer** Peter Porter **Peter Redgrove** Christopher Reid **Vernon Scannell** Penelope Shuttle **Jon Silkin** Ken Smith and **Charles Tomlinson** are represented by up to four poems each in this collection celebrating 15 years of the Beeston Poets readings.

Laughing All the Way by *Liz Cashdan*
0 907123 46 5, 70 pages, £5.99

Includes the acclaimed Tyre-Cairo letters — a dramatic reconstruction of an 11th century Jewish family, which won the *Jewish Quarterly* Wingate Prize.

Five Leaves' books are available from bookshops or, post free, from Five Leaves, PO Box 81, Nottingham NG5 4ER. A full catalogue is available on www.fiveleaves.co.uk.

78